First Tim

CW00485251

The Ultimate Dad's Survival Guide. All
The Tips For Becoming A New Father
For Being Prepared From Pregnancy To
The First Year Of Fatherhood

JOHN RILEY

© Copyright 2022 by JOHN RILEY All rights reserved.

This document is geared towards providing exact and reliable information regarding the topic and issue covered. The publication is sold with the idea that the publisher is not required to render accounting, officially permitted, or otherwise, qualified services. If advice is necessary, legal, or professional, a practiced individual in the profession should be ordered.

- From a Declaration of Principles which was accepted and approved equally by a Committee of the American Bar Association and a Committee of Publishers and Associations.

In no way is it legal to reproduce, duplicate, or transmit any part of this document in either electronic means or printed format. Recording of this publication is strictly prohibited, and any storage of this document is not allowed unless with written permission from the publisher. All rights reserved.

The information provided herein is stated to be truthful and consistent. In terms of inattention or otherwise, any liability, by any usage or abuse of any policies, processes, or directions contained within is the solitary and utter responsibility of the recipient reader. Under no circumstances will any legal responsibility or blame be held against the publisher for reparation, damages, or monetary loss due to the information herein, either directly or indirectly.

Respective authors own all copyrights not held by the publisher.

The information herein is offered for informational purposes solely and is universal as such. The presentation of the information is without a contract or any type of guarantee assurance.

The trademarks used are without any consent, and the publication of the trademark is without permission or backing by the trademark owner. All trademarks and brands within this book are for clarifying purposes only and are owned by the owners, not affiliated with this document.

Contents

Introduction

When fathers can establish good connections with their child's mother and other people in their children's lives then they are more successful as parents. Children learn a lot by watching their parents treat each other with respect and care. This is an opportunity for fathers who did not have excellent role models in their own life to show their children how to be decent men. A good father should be able to handle difficult topics and keep confrontations to a minimum. He should be able to comprehend the difficulties that women encounter so that, as a father, he can assist in the resolution of problems rather than the creation of new ones. He needs to understand how extended family and community members may help youngsters achieve their goals. He should be mature enough to understand how their actions toward adult family members, teachers, and others can help educate their children how to respect others. However, in order to accomplish all of the above, the father must establish his legal paternity. When a kid is born outside of marriage, the biological father has no legal rights or connection to the child unless legal paternity is established. When a child is born within a marriage, whether or not he is the biological father, the male spouse of the mother is immediately identified as having legal paternity. If the couple isn't married and the biological father isn't the mother's spouse, the biological father must go through the steps to establish legal fatherhood. It is impossible to establish legal visitation rights without first establishing and developing paternity. Without legal paternity or visitation rights, a biological father often builds a personal relationship with his kid. That relationship, on the other hand, may be entirely dependent on the mother's discretion. The biological father who has not proven legal paternity as well as legal visitation rights has no legal recourse if the mother decides to stop the father's visits. If the father's name is not on the birth certificate, paternity cannot be verified. As a result, the father has no rights to visitation or custody. As a result, the father has no legal authority over academic, medical, or religious decisions. Child support is a significant source of income for single mothers and their children in this situation. Fathers should indeed be expected to provide for their children. Low-income fathers, on the other hand, frequently struggle to meet this obligation. They might not be able to make enough money. Alternatively, their ability to pay may have shifted as a result of a job loss. When fathers fail to pay, the government intervenes, prompting many low-income fathers to flee in fear. Failure to pay can lead to incarceration. A father's incapacity to take care of financial obligations increases once he is imprisoned. Fathers encounter a variety of problems, ranging from complicated legal systems and financial responsibilities to emotional family relationships. Furthermore, a majority of young as well as low-income fathers lack the life experience, education, confidence, and finances necessary to be successful parents, preserve their health, and obtain decent jobs. The purpose of this book is to help fathers overcome obstacles to responsible fatherhood and help them become good fathers.

Chapter 1: What Is Fatherhood?

1.1 What is Fatherhood?

The state of having one or more children is referred to as fatherhood. Having a son or daughter, spending time with him or her, attending to his or her educational and physical needs, assisting him or her in becoming a confident as well as successful individual, taking him or her to games, and getting to know him or her are all aspects of fatherhood.

1.1.1 Origin of the word Father

Father's Day was first celebrated in Spokane, Washington, in 1910. Today, on the third Sunday of June, this day is commemorated all over the world. The true origin of Father's Day is well known, but what about the origin of the word "Father?" The following languages could give an idea about the origin of the English word father:

- From Middle English: fader

- From Old English: fæder

- From Proto-Germanic: fadēr

- The word "father" is also related to the under mentioned ancient languages: Latin: Pater

- Ancient Greek: πατήρ (patēr)

- Sanskrit: पितृ (pitṛ).

1.1.2 What about the word "dad?"

Around the year 1500, the word "dad" was first documented. According to scholars, the word "dad" is derived from the first noises which children make. "Dad" or "Dada" has a similar sound in various languages and is made up of two consonants that sound same.

- In Irish: Daid

- Chechen: Da

- Czech, Latin and Greek: Tata

- Welsh: Tad

- Lithuanian: Tete

- Sanskrit: Tatah

- Turkmen: Däde

1.2 The primary roles of the father

In almost every culture investigated, for this reason, fathers have played three primary roles: provider, protector, and disciplinarian. While we go through the specifics of each of these tasks, it's important to note that in so many two-parent households today, mothers fulfil these three functions about as much as fathers. Mothers keep their kids secure by fastening seatbelts & securing them inside car seats, as well as supervising computer usage and examining the surroundings for other possible risks. The same as fathers, mothers labor outside of the home to take care of their families. Furthermore, today's mothers are tougher with their children than the previous generations, when the expression "You wait till your dad gets back home" was commonplace. We're highlighting the importance of a father's involvement in a child's life for the sake of his development, but it's also necessary to acknowledge that moms play these duties.

1.2.1 Protector

When a lady is expecting a kid, one of several advised strategies is to encourage males to child-proof or baby-proof their houses. What could they do to get their home ready for the arrival of baby? This is one of the methods fathers can protect their kids against risks in the home. They could also keep their kids secure from the hazards of the outside world. This is particularly important in regions where crime is more prevalent, as the child may be revealed to criminal activity or gangs. The universe is seen through the perspective of mothers who are linked to their children. Fathers have a chance to analyze their children through the lens of how they engage with the outside world. Mom's typical focus is on protecting her child from harm caused by the forces from the outer world (e.g., mean dogs, bullies, accidents, strangers and diseases). This is something she never likes to ever happen to her kid. The paternal impulse in fathers also seeks to prevent unpleasant things from actually happening, but if they can't, they like to do everything they can to make their child to deal with such threats. Dads frequently attempt to prepare their children for external risks such as harmful strangers, vicious pets, lightning, falls, bullies, or accidents. Both of these roles are critical for the child's development. The child is being protected by mom, and the child is being prepared by dad. Fathers also perform the role of guardian by observing the social surroundings and getting to know their children's peers and friends. Also, do we know what is in the home when our children visit another family? Do they have guns in their home? Is it located in a secure area? What do I need to do to safeguard my child from potentially dangerous environments?

Fathers also ensure their children's safety by shaping their surroundings. In other words, they can take a look around (e.g., the house, the neighborhood, the community) and encourage safe activities while also removing potential hazards from the child's path.

1.2.2 Provider

In the role of provider, a father's capacity to look after for his family is tied to his feeling of identity, duty, and manhood. Cultures send different messages regarding what it takes to be a spouse, a male and a father. In most of these cultures, one of the most important duties of the father is that of a provider. That "real men bring home the bacon" that they provide for their families by working in mines, factories, and forests or tending to the fields. Despite the dangers of the tasks, it is their position as the breadwinner of the family that they must fulfil. As previously said, fathers are no longer single breadwinners in many two-parent households, but they continue to play an important role in their families.

1.2.3 Disciplinarian

Fathers frequently have high expectations when it comes to preparing their children for their future. They like their kid to achieve success, to realise what is ahead, and to aspire to better and bigger things. As a result, fathers must be present to educate their children how to control their impulses, keep calm under pressure, and deal with the situations in which they do not risk themselves or others. Many fathers in the United States dominant culture are disciplinarians, but they must do so in a secure and courteous manner. It can't be in a violent fashion, because boys raised in violent households are more likely to perpetrate the violence in their own families. It is critical to employ this position as a disciplinarian, as the father utilizes his own physical presence to teach their kid how to deal with different situations appropriately.

1.3 How do children want to see their fathers?

Men are becoming increasingly involved in parenting. They don't simply act as the family's provider, protector, and disciplinarian. Fatherhood has evolved in recent years, and men are now adopting a variety of new skills as well as values as a result. Fathers have a huge impact on their children's growth. Fathers can learn a lot about themselves by studying how children perceive their fathers. In the United States, for example, elementary school students were asked to define what makes a good father. They were of the view that a good father makes them feel comfortable, a good father can protect his children from harm, a good father works hard to keep the bad guys away, and a good father always listens to Mum. As a result, children's protection and safety become paramount. The study went on to look into how children view their fathers. The youngsters desired to see their fathers, where they could feel strong and protected. They desired comfort and protection from their fathers. Furthermore, they craved for wise and knowledgeable fathers. The idea that "simply being there" may not be enough to impact the children's development and growth. In relation to the developmental needs of children, researchers have established and characterized quite precise qualities or attitudes of fatherhood. Certain traits and qualities are proving to be important in helping children develop into resilient as well as healthy individuals.

Dependability

Fathers should always be there for their children in good times as well as hard times. Being there and correct isn't enough. It's about being available to their children at all times, both in good situations and troublesome circumstances.

Involvement

On a daily basis, fathers should be continuously and intimately involved in their children's life, interests, hopes, and dreams. Fathers must set their distractions aside in order to be curious and attentive.

Compassion

When the child needs it the most, fathers must exhibit compassion, hope, and trust. Compassion is a state of mind or attitude which allows a child to feel more connected to the childhood experience.

Valuing of mother

The father must respect and adore the mother of his children. It's not only about always agreeing with Mom. Valuing a partner is comparable to validating them for who they are and accepting them with all their flaws. Love and respect are demonstrated through actions rather than words, and it teaches the boys and daughters how to be treated.

Empathy

In order to be understanding, present, and engaged, fathers must also have the patience as well as willingness to listen empathically. We may make others feel heard, respected, and valued by putting ourselves in their shoes.

Verbally expressive

Fathers should be able to speak openly, enforce rules, and be tough but fair without insulting or abusing their children.

Act like humans

Fathers should have the courage to admit and accept their mistakes, be open to feedback, and educate their children that growth is a lifelong process. This means that, in order to teach their children to be human, fathers must demonstrate their humanity as often as possible.

Honesty

Honesty and integrity should be taught by the fathers during the entire growth process of their children.

Playfulness

Fun and play should always be used by fathers to communicate their delight in their children. The advantages of fathers playing, particularly rough and tumble play, have been studied. It teaches children to control their emotions and respect limits and boundaries.

Industrious

Fathers must set an example of a positive work ethic as a source of personal fulfilment and satisfaction. This isn't just a work-related trait; it's a useful attitude toward tasks in broad sense.

Chapter 2: Scientific Research on the Importance of Fatherhood

There are scientific reasons why children benefit from having a father figure in their life. There's no denying that parenting techniques have a long-term impact on a child's well-being. However, parenting studies frequently focus on mothers rather than fathers. This casts the subject of how to be a good father into the background. We know so far that children who have a present as well as engaged father are less likely to drop out of school or end up in jail as compared to children who have absent fathers and no other male caregivers or role models. Children who have close relationships with father figures are less likely to engage in high-risk activities and have sex at an early age. When kids grow up, they're more likely to have high-paying careers and good, secure relationships. When fathers take the role of a parent seriously, they have higher IQ test scores by the age of three and have less psychological difficulties throughout their life. The "father effect" refers to all of these advantages of having an involved father. Children do better when their fathers are actively involved with them. According to research, fathers have a vital role in a child's growth. This may appear self-evident with a father holding his baby. Fatherhood is a growing subject of study, as bizarre as that may sound. Scientists are making up for lost time by presenting definitive evidence on the impact of a father on his children. Almost every day, academic journals publish new research showing how males may both assist and hinder their children, as well as how to be a better father. Some of these outcomes are self-evident, such as the fact that ugly divorces are bad for kids. Others, though, are not. Not everyone would guess that the presence of a father figure is associated with a lack of violence in children. Yes, there is. It's hard to believe that having dad around lessens the chance of female delinquency. Yes, it does. The advantages of a paternal presence are referred to as the "father effect." Of course, having a father who is actively involved in his family is always ideal. A minimal amount of time spent together is required, but the quality of the time is more important than the quantity. For example, watching television together isn't going to help much. Fortunately, today's fathers desire to be more active in their children's lives. And society is progressively expecting more of them. It wasn't always like this. That's why it's essential keeping an eye on the growing consensus on the value of fathers at every stage of a child's development. The most important teachers for children are their fathers and moms. Fathers can wonder, "What are my children learning by witnessing them every day — about life in general, morality, how family members should treat one another, about relationships?" On some level, scientists are investigating a new phenomenon. Their findings endorse the fact that could influence how fathers raise their children.

2.1 Fatherhood starts with sperm

Fathers are more than just sperm providers, yet the DNA carried by sperm is crucial. Genetic information is possibly the greatest and most widespread paternal influence. Some fathers are destined to pass on genetic illnesses to their children. Seek genetic type of counseling before conceiving, especially if you're a member of a high-risk group, to reduce your chances of passing on the most devastating disorders. However, when researching the impact parents have on their children, epigenetics — the study of changes in DNA expression caused by lifestyle choices, the environment, and other external variables — may be the most significant aspect to consider. Although we usually blame moms for tampering with the genetic information in their eggs with drugs and alcohol, we didn't know how a father's vices might affect his sperm. We now know that a man's decisions prior to conception can have long-term consequences for his children. According to studies, males who binge drink prior to conception are more likely to have children with congenital cardiac disease and alcohol dependency. Men's poor food habits can result in unfavorable pregnancy outcomes. According to at least one study, fathers who are stressed prior to conception may predispose their children to high blood sugar. We know that the mother's dietary, hormonal, and psychological environment permanently changes organ structure, cellular response, as well as gene expression in her children. However, research suggests that the same is true for fathers: their lifestyle and the maturity might be represented in molecules that affect gene function.

2.2 Good fathers are incubated

Experts rarely encouraged dads to engage in parent groups, participate in childbirth, or care for infants until the 1960s. Fathers were thought to exist to educate their toddlers to walk and their children to play catch, not to handle baby items. However, research over the last two decades suggests that the earlier a father is involved, the better. Researchers stated in a 1997 book on the topic that fathers who actively participate in labor are effectively forming bonds (although one-way interactions) with their children. According to further research, this leads to a greater early bond to the baby. It's debatable whether early attachment to a newborn leads to more serious participation in the long run, but there's plenty of evidence that it does. The authors of a 2011 literature review on male engagement during pregnancy and labor say that fathers who are actively involved and invested in their children before they are born are disproportionately interested in their children's lives after they are born. Furthermore, as multiple studies have demonstrated, increased parental participation leads to improved results for children. Some scientists say that healthy women as well as newborns must return home as soon as possible after delivery, specifically if the father is not permitted to stay in the hospital overnight. This isn't to imply that fathers don't play a role in the growth of their children. They're out for the count until after delivery after their initial genetic contribution. However, the father's influence begins during pregnancy and labor, and its significance cannot be emphasized.

2.3 Good dads and engaged father figures

Before we get into how involved fathers benefit their children (and how uninvolved fathers hurt them), it's necessary to describe what constitutes an engaged, active, and involved father. To begin with, simply showing up is half the battle. Absent fathers are considerably more likely to have a positive impact than fathers who live with their children and take time out of their days to attend significant events. There are few possibilities for fathers who live apart from their children. "Writing letters, making phone calls — even if you're not physically close, knowing your father cares and wants to be involved as much as possible is extremely essential." Purchasing love as a backup isn't a bad idea. There is a lot of evidence that financial support for children has a positive impact on their outcomes. It goes a long way if fathers can provide for their children. It's one thing to be present; it's quite another to be engaged. Children do not benefit from a large amount of interaction. However, it appears that having more high-quality, involved parenting is linked to improved child outcomes. Another important factor is the warmth that the fathers demonstrate for their children. Fathers who spend a lot of time with their children yet are dismissive or insulting have negative consequences. Behaving coldly toward one's children might be a sign of poor fathering. Insulting your children or indulging in negative behaviors are nearly wholly incompatible with being a present as well as engaged father.

2.4 What is a good father to an infant and toddler?

There's a reason why fathers often wonder why they should spend time and energy on infants who won't care or remember anything for at least another couple of years. They don't seem to miss dad much when he leaves, according to all accounts. They're just as happy to see a puppy or an apple as they are to hug their father when he returns home from work. However, it is critical for fathers to see the big picture. These are completely distinct short-term reactions than the long-term effects of having dad around. Infants with their fathers participating in their lives when they were one month old had higher cognitive scores at age one, according to a 1991 research. If their fathers take an active role from birth, preterm infants also score higher at 36 months. In a related study, infants who interacted with their fathers at the age of 9 months experienced similar benefits. The father effect gets much more significant as infants grow into toddlers. Toddlers as well as young children benefit when fathers are involved in regular routines — dinner, playing in the garden — rather than big, one-time visits, according to studies. Dads also appear to have a special touch, with one study claiming that men are better at teaching children to swim than mothers because they are less overprotective and much more inclined to let their children go into the deep end or swim away from them. Sons, according to anecdotal evidence, need their fathers in particular. Scientists discovered that American and Norwegian boys whose fathers were away fighting in World War II during their childhoods had difficulty forming connections as they grew older. Sons who grow up without fathers (or with disengaged fathers) are less popular in preschool, according to similar studies on the subject. In general, the data reveals that as boys gain social abilities, they rely on their fathers more than anybody else. And a major research of over 9,000 adults found that the loss of a parent has a greater impact on sons than on girls, resulting in health issues similar to those reported following an acrimonious divorce. Even very young children require the presence of their fathers. And, contrary to popular belief (and its underlying sexism), girls require them as well, although for different reasons.

2.5 What is a good dad to a daughter?

The father effect is generally similar for boys and girls until they reach puberty, according to most research. Boys and girls who have fathers in their lives perform well and, in some situations, outperform their classmates. However, studies show that when hormones kick in, dads become the arbiters of their children's sexual conduct as well. Teenage daughters are particularly affected, as they take less sexual risks when they have good relationships with their fathers. Several previous studies have discovered a link between poor fathering and girls' sexual outcomes, such as early as well as risky sexual conduct. A distant or disengaged father may influence his daughters' social settings and sexual psychology to encourage unrestrained sexual conduct. A research surveyed 101 sister pairs aged 18 to 36 years old. When one sister grew up with an active, warm father while the other grew up in a broken household or after their father became less engaged, the former grew up to generally avoid casual, unprotected sex while the latter embraced it. Although the study looked at a variety of outside factors, one of the most important correlations between a woman's sexual decision-making and her relationship with her father was how close she felt to him. This was an especially well-controlled study since it allowed researchers to look at how two women with identical DNA and raised in similar environments differed in their sexual risk-taking. Daughters might learn from their disconnected fathers that males don't spend much in long term relationships, therefore they opt for fleeting flings, according to the study. Daughters with disengaged fathers may experience less parental monitoring and are far more prone to associate with sexually promiscuous acquaintances," according to the study. When daughters have a caring, engaged and responsible father they can be saved from these untoward consequences. According to research, involved fathers are those that behave warmly and meaningfully with their children. They're the kind of fathers that assist with homework and show up at sporting events. When it comes to daughters, spending the time to listen to them, learn about their lives, attend major occasions with them, and provide emotional support could help them from engaging in risky sexual conduct early in life. It is not essential for fathers to be perfect.

Making a genuine effort to be present for their daughters, on the other hand, could make a significant difference.

2.6 What happens when dad disappears?

When dad isn't around, there aren't any benefits. There doesn't appear to be much evidence that why fathers do matter for their children if they live far away. Dads who live with their children are more involved; they read books to them and put them to bed. There is a continuous difference in average involvement when comparing resident and non-resident fathers. Children who lose a parent due to death or incarceration suffer more than those who have fathers who are uninvolved. Several studies have looked into the effects of a father's incarceration on his children. Princeton University's Fragile Families Study, which is now following a cohort of 5,000 children born in the United States between 1998 and 2000, is the largest of these efforts. For various reasons, the majority of the children in the study have unmarried parents as well as absentee fathers. One of the most frightening findings of the Fragile Families Study is that when a father is far away, he has very limited power to influence his children positively. When "being away" means being locked up, children face new challenges, perhaps more significant than those they would have encountered if their fathers had died or left because of divorce. The majority of research on widowhood reveals that children whose fathers have died have a better life than children whose parents have divorced. There is a lot of stigma and stress associated with incarceration. When their fathers are incarcerated, it is usually worse on the children.

2.7 How to be a good dad

There's a lot that goes into being a good father. In terms of genetics, it's critical to make healthy choices before conceiving so that your child has the best chance at a life. It's critical to coach your partner during pregnancy and birth so that your bond with your child begins early. Even if your child may never remember, it is as crucial to learn to play with them. One of the most crucial components of fatherhood is advising your teenage daughter on how to make good decisions. However, they are the purely mechanical aspects of fatherhood. In a broader sense, these studies all underscore the necessity of parenting effectively — not merely being present and doing what the studies say, but really caring for your children and demonstrating good behavior. Perhaps most significantly, fathers must understand that their children are constantly watching them and that what they do counts. The quality of a father's parenting has a significant impact on a child's psychological, cognitive, as well as social development, as well as their path to maturity. It's because fathers are always important.

2.8 Engaged fathers play a vital role in the lives of their children

The meaning of father has changed over the years, even as the concept of family has. In households ranging from wedded to recombined, cohabiting, and single parent, 60 % of American men now also have at least one biological kid, and there are biological fathers as well as legal, social, and stepfathers. Three-quarters of fathers in the United States have more than one biological kid, and three-quarters of children live with their parents or only their father. Regardless of the fact that they are even not legally recognized as father figures, most men serve as such. The emphasis of social science study has shifted as well, from just how the absence of father affects children's development to the consequences of father engagement. Similarly, social assistance programming is shifting away from a mother-centered focus and toward options that include as well as welcome men. Different scientific research is investigating and exploring the existing facts and hypotheses about how helpful, engaged fathers are related to their children's healthy development.

There is increasing consensus that involved the fathers' situation

Involved type of fathering is defined as affectionate, sensitive, supportive, friendly, close, warm, friendly, comforting, nurturing, encouraging, and accepting fathering. Fathers who participate in their children's lives have a positive impact on them from the minute they are born. Having a supportive spouse throughout pregnancy is associated to less maternal health issues and better results for both the mother and the baby. According to the study, paternal prenatal attachment has also been connected to advantages in the father-kid relationship. The structure of a couple's relationship often determine how both the parents will react to their child's needs, and dads' supportive (or abusive) behavior can have an impact on maternal bonding to their newborn. According to numerous studies, children who have caring, involved fathers have greater academic performance, school readiness, greater math as well as verbal skills, stronger emotional security, higher levels of self-esteem, fewer behavioral problems, & greater social skills than kids that do not have the involved, caring fathers. These findings back up a growing body of evidence in study, practice and policy that indicates that engaged fathers have a distinctive and important impact on their kid's development. However, many biological fathers no longer survive with their children as a result of the drop in marriages, rise in separation, and rise in non-marital childbearing on the last half-century, limiting interaction. Nonresident fathers having a positive co-parenting connection with their children's mothers are more engaged in their children's lives. Numerous studies have linked paternal absence to negative implications for the well-being of their children. Children of participating fathers are more prone to become the involved mom and dad themselves, according to studies. Girls place a high priority on their fathers as well. According to a study, women who grew up with the involved dad had less psychiatric disorders as adults than the women who actually did not.

Newer models of fatherhood are being used to examine fathers' core functions

As social scientists' attention turned from the father's absence to the father's involvement, a more comprehensive perspective of paternal engagement was required, covering what and actually how much dads do with and for their children. Consequently, the "Involved Model of Fatherhood" has become the prevailing frame. It is divided into three sections:

Positive engagement

Fathers who are completely involved have positive interactions with their kids, including providing care like changing the diapers and participating in shared activities such as play.

Accessibility

It is important to note that involved fathers remain accessible to their kids even when they are not physically interacting with their children and are involved in cooking or other chores.

Responsibility

Fathers who are actively involved bear ultimate duty for their children's care and welfare, which includes participating in child-rearing decisions and also making sure that their

children's needs are satisfied on a continuous basis.

Fathers unique value could be ascertained only by comparative analysis of father and mother involvement

Mothers are generally associated with protection and nurturing, while the significance of fathers is disputed (although the financial provider is more commonly seen as a central). Fathers are more engaged into play than moms are in caring for their children, and their playing is more physically demanding. Fathers generally encourage their kids to take chances and be self-sufficient, while mothers emphasize the importance of avoiding danger and injury. A relatively new branch of the fatherhood research investigates how fathers motivate their children to overcome challenges, discover, take risks, be brave in the stranger's presence, & advocate for themselves.

Researchers are studying family structures as well as transitions

Many academics are investigating whether family arrangements and transitions, like intact social-father, biological-parent, or single-parent households, are connected with children's behavior and academic achievement during the middle childhood. For instance, one research looked at the link between the length of primary- time-school-aged kids spend inside a structure of a certain family and their behavior and academic achievement. There were no variations in the children's early well-being all among the various household types, according to the researchers. They did, however, notice significant changes in children's state of happiness over time. Kids who spend their whole childhood, including both the biological parents, perform better academically and have fewer behavioral problems than children who actually spend time with other types of families.

Policymakers and involved fathers' vital role inside their children's lives

The increasing body of data demonstrates that being an involved father is beneficial to children's development. Academic behavior, achievement, and social interaction are less problematic for children who seem to have a father who is actively engaged in their lives than for children that do not have a dad who is actively engaged in their lives. Practitioners and policymakers are aiming to find for methods to incorporate dads in programming in order to successfully educate, teach, and groom their children.

Chapter 3: Start by Planning a Family with Your Spouse

Whether you're fantasizing of lovely little toes and fingers or just struggling to figure to see which birth control option is good for you, family planning conversations are an important aspect of a relationship of long-term. This is undoubtedly true for individuals who don't want kids, those who desire a huge family, and those that already have kids and are thinking about adding to their family. The effectiveness of these conversations involves understanding when to exactly have the baby chat and what kind of questions to address.

3.1 Dos and Dont's of planning a family

Before you attempt to plan a family with your partner you should weigh all the consequences. This means that you should know about all the dos and don'ts of planning a family with your amazing partner.

Dos of family planning

You can control the amount of children you have and the time between their births by using family planning. Modern medicine gives you the flexibility and independence you need, whether you want to start trying for a baby right away or want to focus on your job and put off parenting for a few years. Here are a few pointers on how to address the situation effectively.

Communicate with your partner

Always be open and honest about your goals and expectations with your partner. Whether you want to focus on your work and passion first or you're ready to start family planning right away, making sure you're on the exact page helps alleviate any stress or anxiety.

Start the conversation

What you say isn't always as crucial as how you begin the conversation. As a result, establishing a comfortable environment for open and honest conversation is a crucial initial step. Talking regarding family planning demands a comfortable environment where both the partners, even if they aren't on the exact page, may be heard and understood. This might be as easy as inquiring if this is a great time to talk about something important before getting started. To start out family planning talk, it's best to let one partner speak first, so they may express their thoughts and needs. The best statements are those that begin with "I." Start your statements with expressions such as "I feel..." or "I am afraid..." You can show that you understand by confirming your partner's point of view, even if it differs from your own. "It's understandable that you'd feel that way since...", for example. Then exchange roles and also let the other person listen and validate. If you do have a feeling you and your spouse aren't on the exact page, it's a good idea to establish realistic type of expectations right away. The purpose of the discussion should be to ensure that both you and your partner feel seen and understood, rather than making this momentous decision right away.

Investigate all your options

Family planning is now easier and even more versatile than it has ever been because of the medical advancements. The IUD, pills, and hormone shots are just a few of the birth control alternatives available. On the other hand, advances in technology such as IVF make it simpler to overcome infertility. Look into the tools you'll need to achieve your objectives.

Be on the exact page

It's important to remember that also there are a variety of valid explanations for not having children or a lack of desire to form a family. Many people are afraid of losing their independence, others are afraid of not being a great parent, and still others simply require more time together before starting a family. That is why it is critical for couples to take their time to hear to one another's concerns about becoming parents. As a relationship progresses, family planning must ideally become a topic of discussion. Imagine yourself being in the long-term relationship or marriage and bringing up the subject of having kids only to discover that your spouse is opposed to it. Couples who are honest and open early on in their relationship are more likely to stay on the exact page as a relationship grows. Couples counseling is always recommended if you're having problems with family planning discussion or negotiating the parenthood process. Couples could go through a thrilling but difficult time, and having a counselor guide a few of these discussions can be quite helpful.

Brainstorm the questions

Before you sit together, think of some topics and questions you'd like to address with your spouse. If you're not sure where to begin or what questions to ask, consider starting with the following:

- What's your thoughts on having kids?

- What is the strength of your stance on this?

- When it comes to having a child, what is "enough" money?

- What's your thoughts on abortion, genetic testing, and birthing methods?

- What matters most when it comes to being a mother or father? Are there any exceptional instances in your life that you would cherish?

- What are the components of kid care that you value the most? What about education, whether private, public, or homeschooling?

- How would we maintain our romance after that we have a child?

- How would we strike a balance between life and work?

- How would you like to manage special occasions such as holidays and birthdays?

- If at all, how would we approach spirituality or religion?

These all questions may be useful in starting a discussion regarding family planning. If you and your partner decide you want to start a family, it's time to delve deeper into the more common subjects that come up during these discussions.

Set standards for your relationship

It's a good idea to talk about how to prioritize your relationship during the changes before you have a baby. Couples with young children must be extra deliberate about making time for each other.

When a cooing baby enters the picture, a lot of attention is naturally redirected.

Need to work on creating a shared vision of the future

Although it may feel like a long way off, developing a common vision for your family's future is an important part of the family planning process. Try this simple exercise: Make a list of the steps you want to take right now to get ready for the future you want.

Discuss the hot topics from the outset

Discipline, child care and religion are just a few of the topics that elicit strong emotional reactions. To avoid unpleasant shocks later on, it's a good idea to bring these issues up immediately.

Diaper duty

There will undoubtedly be enough time to go through all of the finer points. Getting on the exact page over how household chores would be shared once the baby arrives can help you avoid disappointment in the future.

Discuss relationship health

"How strong does our relationship feel today?" is one question each partner must ask themselves and each other. In certain cases, couples in distress conceive a child in the hopes of reconciling or mending their relationship. If you're at this point in your relationship, prenuptial or couples counseling may be beneficial to improve your bond before starting a family. Babies can provide happiness and pleasure to a relationship that is already strained, but

they can also increase stress. So working to strengthen your foundation prior to bringing home kid would be beneficial to you.

Consider current challenges

Consider the activities that are currently posing a daily challenge. Is there a fair division of duties with regard to child care, emotional labor, and other responsibilities? When it comes to coaching your toddler, do you agree?

Avoid outside pressure

Although the decision to have additional children is a personal one, it does not prevent others from expressing their opinions. The temptation to make a decision about future children doesn't go away after having a baby, whether it's feeling like the only parent at preschool who isn't expecting baby number two or coping with comments about your biological clock. When discussing your family, keep in mind that what's best for others, such as your in-laws and friends, isn't always best for you.

Give yourself time

Perhaps you've always wanted to be a young parent, or perhaps you're a few years older and believe this is your only chance. Whatever the circumstance, it can feel as if this decision had to be made yesterday, which can be stressful. Keep in mind that you can create your own schedule. Whether that means revisiting the topic in a few months or a few years is irrelevant. If you need more time, find a birth control method that fits your schedule and take a vacation from thinking about babies for a while.

3.2 Don'ts of family planning

Given below are the dont's of family planning:

Go through it alone

Perhaps you're taking IVF treatments, or perhaps you're expecting your first kid and are apprehensive about parenthood. There's no need to go through these things alone. There are numerous methods to connect with others who may empathize with you and offer assistance, ranging from infertility support groups to parenting programs.

Don't be reluctant in consulting a professional

Always consult a professional if you have any questions or concerns. Family members and friends can provide emotional support, but everyone's situation is different. You want expert medical advice tailored to your specific physical needs, tastes, and objectives. An obstetrics team will have the resources needed to conduct testing, identify the source of any problems, and propose effective treatments.

Smoking/Alcohol/Substance Abuse

It would be great if you and your partner quit smoking for the sake of you and the baby. Miscarriages, preterm birth, low birth weight, and stillbirth can all be caused by smoking during pregnancy. Chest infections, cough, and Sudden Infant Death Syndrome are more common in babies whose parents smoke. Excessive drinking might decrease sperm production and result in impotence. The safest way is to avoid drinking at all before and throughout pregnancy. Women who get pregnant unintentionally are concerned about binge drinking prior to conception. A single binge drinking incident is unlikely to do harm to the baby. While trying to conceive and throughout the pregnancy, psychoactive substance usage must be avoided.

Medications

The baby's development takes place mostly during the first three months of pregnancy. As a result, all medications (including over-the-counter drugs) must be avoided during this time, with the exception of critical medicines. Tell your doctor if you're planning a pregnancy and are taking regular drugs for a medical condition.

Chapter 4: Guideline from Pregnancy to Arrival of Baby

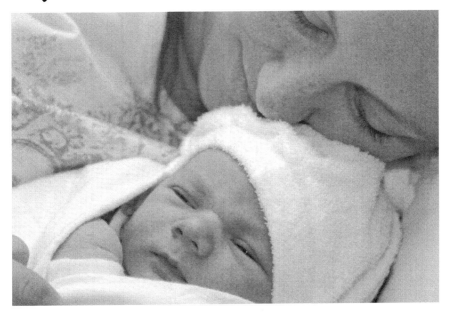

After you and your partner have decided about having a baby, there are steps which need to be taken for safe and secure conception of the child.

4.1 Pregnancy Test

The very first day of your partner's most recent menstrual period marks the start of pregnancy. The age of gestational, also known as menstruation age, is the age at which a woman becomes pregnant. It's roughly two weeks before fertilization actually takes place. Although it may appear unusual, the very first day of your partner's last menstruation will be a crucial milestone in establishing your deadline. This date will be brought up by your healthcare professional, who will utilize it to determine how far along in your pregnancy are you? One week after your partner's missed period is the optimal time to take a pregnancy test. This is the most effective approach to avoid a false negative result. In women who have regular/predictable monthly menses, home pregnancy tests can be utilized as early as the first day after your partner's first missed period. Because identifying your partner's exact moment of ovulation is tricky, you can have her administer a test two weeks after intercourse if she has irregular cycles. Human chorionic gonadotropin (HCG) is a hormone generated in early pregnancy that is identified by pregnancy tests. This hormone is produced gradually and rises as the pregnancy progresses. When the HCG level reaches 20-50 milliunits/milliliters, standard urine pregnancy tests will detect it. If your spouse takes a test too soon, the levels of HCG may not be high enough to detect a pregnancy, resulting in a false negative, even if she is pregnant.

4.2 How to prevent a false negative result

Taking the test too soon after your partner conceives is the most common cause of a false negative test. Additionally, if you do not carefully follow the test instructions, your partner's result may be affected. Even if a woman drinks a lot of water, she should still get a positive urine test. However, before undergoing a test, urine should not be diluted with water. When the partner first wakes up in the morning, it's a terrific moment to take the test. If a test comes out negative in a woman who thinks she's pregnant or has irregular periods, she should take another test in a week.

Medications and test results

Medications rarely interfere with test findings, creating neither false positives nor false negatives. Only HCG-containing medications would have an impact on the outcome.

When to visit the doctor

Although home tests can detect a pregnancy, they provide no information on the viability of the pregnancy. It's critical to schedule an appointment with the doctor to confirm the partner's pregnancy and have an ultrasound to identify a fetal heart rate (usually at six to 10 weeks). If the partner has a positive pregnancy test, the obstetrician can tell you about the warning indications of an abnormal or worrisome pregnancy and when to schedule an appointment to confirm it.

4.2.1 How soon can you know that your partner is pregnant?

From the moment of conception, the (hCG) hormones human chorionic gonadotrophin will be circulating in the partner's bloodstream. This hormone is produced by the cells that produce the placenta (food sources for the increasing fetus). It's also the same hormone detected by a pregnancy test. Although this hormone is there from the beginning, it requires a while for it to accumulate in your partner's body. After the very first day of your spouse's last menstruation, the hCG level rises sufficiently to be detected by pregnancy tests, which takes 3 to 4 weeks.

4.2.2 When should you contact the healthcare provider regarding a new pregnancy?

To make your first appointment, contact your healthcare practitioner after the partner has a pregnancy test that is positive. Your healthcare practitioner may inquire if your spouse is getting a prenatal vitamin when you call. Folic acid is present in several supplements. During pregnancy, it's critical that your partner consumes around 400 micrograms of folic acid per day to ensure that the fetus' neural tube (the beginning of the spine and brain) grows properly. Even if your spouse is not pregnant, many healthcare practitioners recommend that pregnant women take folic acid-fortified prenatal vitamins. If your spouse did not take prenatal vitamins prior to becoming pregnant, your doctor may advise her to begin as soon as possible.

Fetal Development

During a regular pregnancy, the fetus actually will undergo significant changes. Trimesters are three stages in which time is distributed. Each trimester lasts around three months. Your healthcare professional will most likely refer to development of fetal in weeks. So, if your partner has been pregnant for three months, she is roughly 12 weeks. Pregnancy is often thought to be a 9-month process. This isn't always the scenario, though. A 40-week (280-day) pregnancy is considered full-term. Your partner can be pregnant for 9 months or ten months, depending on the months she is pregnant and the week she gives birth. This is perfectly acceptable and healthy behavior.

4.3 Stages of Growth Month-by-Month in Pregnancy

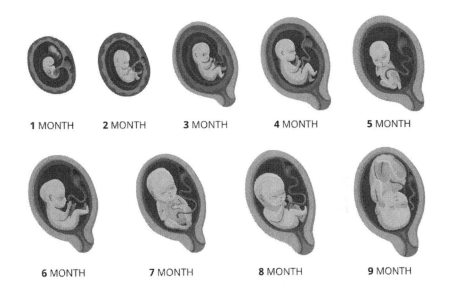

1 MONTH 2 MONTH 3 MONTH 4 MONTH 5 MONTH

6 MONTH 7 MONTH 8 MONTH 9 MONTH

You should be aware of the following growth stages so that you can properly take care of your partner and be aware of the approximate time of delivery of your child.

First trimester

The first trimester lasts between conception to 12 weeks. This usually happens throughout the very first 3 months of pregnancy. During this trimester, the fertilized egg will evolve from a tiny cluster of cells to a fetus with baby-like traits.

Month 1 (weeks one through four)

During this trimester, the placenta develops. The placenta is a flat, spherical organ that carries nutrients and waste from the mom to the fetus. During your pregnancy, regard the placenta as the source of nutrients for the fetus. During the first few weeks, face which is primitive with the huge dark circles for eyes will emerge. The lower jaw, throat and mouth are all developing. Circulation will start as blood cells begin to form. The fetus is about ¼-inch long by the first month end, roughly the size of a grain of rice.

Month 2 (weeks 5 to 8)

The development of facial features continues. Each ear starts as a tiny fold of skin on the head's side. Tiny buds are forming, which will eventually expand into legs and arms. The formation of toes, fingers, and eyes is also underway. The neural tube (spinal cord, brain, and any other central nervous system neural tissue) is now fully formed. In addition, the digestive tract and the sensory organs start to mature. Cartilage is being replaced by bone. It's referred to as a fetus by medical professionals rather than an embryo after the eighth week.

Month 3 (weeks 9 to 12)

The feet, arms, fingers, hands, and toes have all completed their development. The fetus is now beginning to explore its surroundings by closing and opening its hands and lips. The external ears are forming, and toenails and fingernails are starting to emerge. Under the gums, the first teeth are growing. The reproductive organs develop as well, although ultrasonography still makes gender identification problematic. The fetus is fully formed by the third month end. All the organs & limbs (extremities) are there and will develop further in order to become operational. The urinary and circulatory systems are both working, and bile is produced by the liver. After three months, your partner's likelihood of miscarriage lowers significantly because the most crucial development has completed.

Second trimester

The third trimester of the pregnancy is frequently regarded as the most enjoyable journey part. Morning sickness should have passed by this point, as well as the discomforts of the early pregnancy. During this month, the fetus will begin to develop face features. As the fetus turns and twists into the uterus, your partner may start to experience movement as well. Many people learn whether their new born will be female or male at birth during this trimester. This is usually done around 20 weeks when doing the anatomy scan. You can plan for the new baby's clothes and other needs based on the results of this scan.

What to expect- Month 4 (weeks 13 to 16)

The toes and fingers are clearly defined. Eyelids, brows, nails, eyelashes, and hair are all created during this process. Bones and teeth become denser. The fetus can even suck her or his thumb, stretch, yawn, and make the faces while still inside the womb. Then nervous system is beginning to work. The reproductive organs as well as genitalia have fully matured, as well as your doctor can use ultrasound to determine whether the fetus will be born female or male.

Month 5 (weeks 17 to 20)

Your partner may notice the fetus circulating about at this point. The fetus is growing and exercising its muscles. Quickening is the first movement, which can seem like the flutter. The fetus is around 10-inches long & weighs around 1/2 to around 1 pound by the end of the fifth month.

Month 6 (weeks 21 to 24)

The skin of fetus is reddish in color, wrinkled, and veins are apparent through translucent skin if you could see the inside of the uterus right now. Fingerprints and toe prints can be observed. At this point, the eyelids start to part as well as the eyes open. The fetus begins to move or increases its pulse in response to sounds. If the fetus has the hiccups, you may observe jerking motions. If your baby is born early, he or she may survive if given urgent care following 23rd week.

Month 7 (weeks 25 to 28)

The fetus continues to grow and create body fat cell reserves. At this point, your hearing is fully matured. The fetus moves around a lot and reacts to stimuli like pain, sound, and light. If your kid is born prematurely, after the seventh month, there's a good chance of survival for them.

Third trimester

This is where your partner's pregnancy comes to an end. You might be enticed to start counting the days till your partner's due date in the expectation that it would come sooner, but every week of this last period of development aids the fetus in preparing for birth. During third trimester, the fetus rapidly acquires weight, accumulating body fat in the body that will be useful after the birth. Keep in mind that, despite the fact that popular culture only acknowledges 9 months of pregnancy, your partner could be pregnant for up to ten months. A full-term of pregnancy lasts forty weeks, which means your spouse will be pregnant for the tenth month. It's also likely that you'll be able to go a week or two past your deadline (forty-one or forty-two weeks). As your partner near her own due date, your own healthcare professional will keep a careful eye on her. If she doesn't go into unprompted labor after her due date, your provider may decide to induce her. This means that drugs will be utilized to induce labor and give birth to your child. Throughout this trimester, make sure to discuss the plan of birth with your own healthcare practitioner.

Month 8 (weeks 29 to 32)

The fetus continues to grow and create body fat cell reserves. It's possible that you'll notice more kicking. At this stage, the fetus's brain is quickly developing, and it can hear and see. Internal systems majority are mature, but the lungs might be immature.

Month 9 (weeks 33 to 36)

The fetus continues to develop and grow throughout this time. The lungs are practically fully developed at this very point. Blinking, shutting eyes, turning the head, grasping firmly, and responding to light, sounds, and touch are all reflexes that the fetus has developed.

When the baby will be at Home-Month 10 (Weeks 37 to 40)

Your partner could enter into the labor at any point during the last month. Because space is limited, your partner may notice less movement. The fetus' posture may have shifted at this very point to get ready for the birth. It should be head down in your partner's uterus if possible. As the fetus descends into her pelvis and get ready for birth, your partner may feel very uneasy in this final stretch of time. At this moment, the new born is ready to actually meet the rest of the world. They are approximately 18 to 20 inches long and weigh approximately 7 pounds.

4.4 To-do list for fathers while getting ready for baby and after the baby's arrival into the world

Right now, the partner may be getting the most of the attention, but once your new kid arrives, you'll both have your hands full. Also, check with your doctor — or your partner's doctor — about any other steps you might take to ensure a healthy pregnancy. If you're a smoker, for example, do everything you can to quit. Secondhand smoking contains chemicals that can harm your baby both before and after delivery.

The Birth

It can be frightening to think about your baby's birth. You can, however, do a lot to make things move more smoothly.

- A childbirth class can teach you the fundamentals

- Discuss pain management with your partner during delivery

- Learn massage techniques to assist your partner during labor and delivery.

- Take a tour of the hospital where your baby will be born

- Have a route of the facility that is the most efficient

- Make a list of key phone numbers and program them into your phone

- If you have other children, make childcare arrangements for the time of the birth

- Make a list of people who should be notified when the baby is born

How can you help your partner during pregnancy?

Your partner will most likely want you to stay with them for support. Then you should decide how active you will be together. Take into account both of your personalities, how you interact with one another, and what you expect from labor and delivery as a couple. In an ideal world, they'd get the aid they need, and you'd pitch in at a level that's comfortable for you. There are some of the roles for fathers. Any of them will suffice as long as it is convenient for both of you.

Be a coach

This is the most active part of the job. You'll support and encourage your partner, as well as act as their advocate with the hospital staff. You may be able to lift the baby out and place it on their belly in some situations. You'll learn about each stage of labor, how your partner might feel or act during it, and how to guide them through breathing as well as relaxation exercises in childbirth classes. Childbirth classes, no matter how involved you want to be, can help you understand what to anticipate and put your mind at ease about childbirth.

Share the coaching

For both of you, labor can be a lengthy and arduous process. You might want to take the support of a friend or family member. This someone can assist with the coaching and remain with your spouse when you need to eat or take a break. An additional person can help you both emotionally and physically.

Be a teammate

You might enjoy this role if you want to be involved in the game but don't want to quarterback. You offer support and encouragement when your spouse asks, but you prefer to let them or the nurses tell you what to do and how much to do. You could want to engage a doula, a trained labor "caregiver," in this scenario. Doulas are usually advocates for patients and hands-on coaches. When the nurse needs to leave for an extended period of time, a doula stays with you. A doula can help you concentrate on your partner and the birth.

Cheer from the sidelines

This is a popular choice among couples. You are supposed to touch your partner's back and hold their hand. You can take picture or videotape your baby's birth. It's even possible to sever the umbilical cord. But you are content to delegate the specialist job to the people who can perform it well.

Wait outside

In some circumstances, a mother does not want the father of her child present. There's a big possibility they won't if you weren't involved with the pregnancy or if you're estranged from them. If your presence in the room makes them feel stressed for whatever reason, it might make labor and delivery more challenging. Then it's preferable for you to be somewhere else. Being with their partner, on the other hand, is a good decision for most dads. In one survey, 81 percent of new fathers reported the experience was fulfilling and joyful. Irrespective of how involved you want to be, witnessing your child's final push into the globe may be an unforgettable event.

Home and Car

Your partner's energy level may be low right now. You can help a lot by preparing your home and car for your newborn.

- Prepare the nursery.

- Baby-proof your home.

- Prepare some meals and store them in the freezer.

- Put your baby's car seat in place.

- If childcare or housework assistance is required, ensure that it is simply get done by you.

Work and Finances

By putting the financial ducks in a row, you may put your mind at peace. It is never too early to begin making plans for the future.

- Consider paternity leave.

- Arrange for family health insurance.

- Speak with a financial planner about your options.

- If you can, establish a college or special fund.

Baby Care and Bonding

Your child will be fortunate to have both of you. Now is an excellent moment to learn everything you can about parenting in this strange new world.

- Enroll with your spouse in parenting classes.

- Discover how bonding can be aided by holding and feeding.

- Learn how to change diapers so that your partner may get some rest.

- Choose some of your favorite childhood books to read to the child.

- Inquire about well-baby checkups.

- Prepare for the years ahead by learning about child development.

Life with your partner

Your companion is surely fragile after the difficulties of childbirth. They may be painful for several weeks after giving birth, whether via vaginally or C-section and may endure some bleeding & vaginal discharge. Urination can be unpleasant, and urinary incontinence (unintentional urine leakage) might occur. As a consequence of strain of delivery, they may develop hemorrhoids or constipation. If they gave birth vaginally and suffered a vaginal tear, the bleeding could last longer. Following a C-section, they must restrict their movement for a few weeks. These days, it's enough to have anyone enraged. The following actions should be taken:

- Make as much of a contribution as feasible.

- Help out around the house by doing the heavy lifting, such as grocery laundry, shopping, & meal preparation.

- Patience is very important, especially when it arrives to physical contact. It might take up to six weeks for them to recover fully, and even then, individuals may not be ready for sexual activity. Allow them to lead the way, and show your love with kisses and hugs. They might also appreciate a good foot rub every now and again.

Breastfeeding may not be a breeze

Breastfeeding isn't simple for all moms and babies, despite the fact that it appears to be a natural process. If your infant is having problems feeding, your partner may become frustrated. Your partner's nipples may be painful at first as they learn to latch on properly. Clogged milk ducts can be an unpleasant problem for some women. Mom isn't getting much sleep either, because the baby needs to eat every two to three hours. You can assist your partner by doing the following:

- Make them **sleep** when the baby sleeps.

- Consider it your responsibility and job to manage nighttime diaper changes.

Emotional changes

The "baby blues" are a type of sadness and anxiety experienced by some new mothers. It's natural to feel unhappy, anxious, or despondent while you adjust to motherhood. However, if these feelings worsen, become severe, or persist longer than a few weeks, they may be suffering from postpartum depression, which they should discuss with their doctor. You can assist your partner by doing the following:

- If you see they've been down, inquire about their feelings. Just conversing with you could be quite beneficial.

- Encourage them to take breaks and get out of the house while you look after the baby, even if it's only for a few minutes.

- Encourage them to get help if they exhibit symptoms of postpartum depression. They might not even realize they're depressed.

Keep in mind that this is only a temporary situation. Your partner will feel more like themselves again before you realize it, your baby will start sleeping for longer periods of time, and you'll all settle into a normal schedule as a new family.

Physical intimacy during pregnancy

Welcome to pregnancy, when many couples discover that their sex life has turned into a roller coaster, with neither partner knowing what to expect from one other. Pregnancy may cut deep into a couple's private lives, from raging hormones and mood swings to terrible weariness, a change in body image, worries, anxiety, and sometimes, essential medical reasons not to make love. It's not uncommon to discover many couples splitting apart at the emotional seams at a time when they should be pulling closer together. Every sense of intimacy appears to come to a halt at times, and neither partner knows why. Don't worry if this sounds familiar. While having sex — specifically, having intercourse — may be out of the question for a part or possibly the entirety of the pregnancy, intimacy does not have to suffer. Experts suggest that all it takes is a minor shift in mindset and a rethinking of what it means to be close to your mate. Too often, couples believe that if they can't have intercourse for any reason, they might as well just stay away from each other completely and eliminate the concept of intimacy from the minds. Instead, couples must accept that intercourse and orgasm are only one way to experience intimacy and that if that isn't possible, there are other ways to stay close. Even if there isn't any intercourse, stroking and caressing, and even just getting nude together and communicating how that vulnerability feels, can help maintain intimacy links strong between lovers.

During all phases of a typical pregnancy, sex is considered safe. Obviously, just because it's safe to have sex when pregnant doesn't indicate you'll want to. Many pregnant moms notice that their interest for sex alters as the pregnancy progresses. In addition, many women discover that as their own bodies become larger, sex becomes uncomfortable. When it comes to your sexual connection, keep the channels of communication open between you and your companion. Discuss additional ways to meet your intimacy needs, like kissing, touching, and cuddling each other. You may also need to try out different sex positions to locate the ones that are most comfortable for you. Many pregnant women lose their Interest and enthusiasm for sex late during the pregnancy, not just due to their size, and also because they are obsessed with the impending delivery and also the joy of becoming the new parent. The uterus' muscular muscles and the amniotic sac (a skinny bag that holds the fetus and associated fluid) protect the newborn from the impacts of sex. A thick mucus barrier also shuts and protects the cervix from infection. The penis doesn't really make contact with fetus during intercourse. Orgasm or intercourse, on the other hand, does not result in contractions or miscarriage. Because semen includes a component that may actually promote contractions, health care doctors also urge that every woman avoid having intercourse during the last trimester of pregnancy as a precautionary measure. Consult your doctor to see what she or he believes is the best option.

Communication is the key

Couples must not underestimate the power of personal discussion in sparking feelings of love. It's intimacy when you talk regarding your hopes, dreams, anxieties, longings, and hidden wishes, especially in a private context. This strengthens the intimate bond that exists and also maintains emotional connection between a woman and a man. That appears to be a plan that is reasonable. However, as any expectant woman knows, the moment she places her head over her partner's shoulder or requests that intimate, bonding cuddles, her thoughts quickly descend below the waist. The woman rejects them, within minutes, they become enraged, and both the partners feel guilty and terrible. So, where did things go wrong? According to experts, the problem stems from a communication lack. The important thing is that the woman makes it clear to her partner that refusing to engage in sexual activity does not imply that she rejects him or even their relationship. The truth is that she's merely focused on their kid for a short period of time, which explains why there's so much biology going on, at least few of them are influencing her feelings regarding the possibility of having sexual intercourse at any time.

When Mum is hot & Dad is not

While it's common for the pregnant companion to be averse to having sex, this isn't always the situation. In reality, even when they're ready to go, it's often the male who has confusing thoughts about intimacy and intercourse and pulls away out of the relationship. The solution to this difficulty is to set aside the "mother" picture, even if only for a short while. For a man, a woman who only thinks totally of herself as 'mommy' and then presents herself as 'mommy' — and even if he only thinks of her as 'mommy' — can be a major turnoff to intimacy. Both partners have a better chance of continuing to relate to one another in the identical intimate way they did before conception, without or with intercourse, if the woman persists to see herself as sexual human being & recognizes that most men actually find their pregnant associates extremely sexy at every size and stage. Many experts think that section of what keeps intimacy intact is for both the partners to maintain the sexual link they've already created, as well as to try to meet the physical requirements of each other when they emerge. This may mean giving to her that exquisite foot rub without going beyond the ankles if that's exactly what she requires right now; for the woman, it could mean understanding her partner's requirements for climax and assisting him in whatever manner she can, even if it doesn't involve intercourse. It's not exactly about pushing yourself to do something you don't like to do; it's about doing your best to meet the requirements of someone you care about. Perhaps most importantly, acknowledge that coupling is regarding the partnership, and that a successful partnership has several components that must be valued in order to maintain intimacy. Our culture, for some reason, does not teach us that the marriage is more than a love relationship, and does not emphasize the aspect of life-partnership. When it comes to creating a living with someone, there are so many equally significant factors to consider. It's all about sacrificing without losing oneself after the day to keep the relationship alive. You should just not give more than you might bear, but you should give each other something.

Ways to Maintain Intimacy During Pregnancy

The following suggestions for pregnancy and beyond can help you preserve the intimacy and romance in your relationship.

Don't take sex or each other for granted

When you initially start dating, you don't anticipate sex to be present at all times; instead, you regard the person in such a way that your hopes are realized. As with dating, you should treat your companion with respect during pregnancy.

Flirting should be revived

Marriage indeed is a multitasking endeavor. As the marriage progresses and practical life concerns arise, you have a tendency to let go of things that began it all, such as flattery, courting, and flirtation. To maintain intimacy, bring back all of the things you actually did to each other before the marriage & flirt like mad.

At least once a week, have a date night.

Couples must set aside time to be together that is solely focused on each other, something that should be continued after the baby is delivered.

Every now and again, surprise your partner.

Expose your companion to something they aren't familiar with — or something they didn't realize you knew about. Alternatively, do something unexpected, such as obtaining a sexual film to rent or taking together a candlelit bat. Create it as a surprise and choose something that both of you enjoy.

Pursue your pregnant wife

Pamper her with the exact delicacy with which you treated her when you initially started dating. It won't make much of a difference to you, but it will make a tremendous difference to her, and it will help out you both stay close.

4.5 Tips to go through the period of pregnancy without stress and with serenity

For both you and your partner, pregnancy may be a stressful time. It's excellent for you, your partner, and your baby if you can develop strategies to cope with stress.

How to turn this period into one of the most beautiful time of your life and not into a time of stress and confusion

Most people are aware that anxiety and sadness can strike women during their pregnancy and the early stages of parenthood, but males are equally vulnerable. Up to one out of every ten new fathers may go through depression during or after the birth of their child. Men's depression isn't always the consequence of their companion experiencing comparable emotions. Whilst mothers with postnatal depression may imply that the father is suffering from it as well, this is not always the case. Depression and anxiety in new fathers can start during pregnancy and worsen after the child is born. New fathers do not have access to the same services as new mothers. They are less likely to visit their doctor, midwife, or mother and child health nurse all of whom can detect problems in women. Depression in the fathers, like depression in women, must be treated and detected early and efficiently. This will assist the father's mental health as well as his relationships with his children, partner, friends and family in the long run.

What might make new fathers depressed?

There are a variety of social, physical, and emotional reasons that can bestow to males getting depression, just as there are with all forms of depression:

- insufficient emotional and social support

- relationship and stress changes

- grief and loss concerns

- difficulties adjusting to the parenthood

- a lack of sleep

- a painful or poor delivery experience

Few men might find it difficult to adjust to changes in their family structure and home life. Men are more less inclined to talk regarding how they actually feel because of traditional beliefs toward parenthood and masculinity. Worries about more obligations, financial strains, and job management can all have an impact.

Risk factors for the paternal depression

Men of all ages, personality types, and socioeconomic situations can be affected by paternal depression. The following are some of the famous risk factors for dads' depression (paternal depression):

- a woman's partner suffering from postpartum depression

- a depression history in the past

- feelings of inadequacy in the parenthood role

- issues with relationships

- low self-esteem

- an unsettled baby

- first-time fatherhood

Symptoms of the paternal depression

Given below are few symptoms that are linked with the postnatal depression in men:

- tiredness

- anger and **anxiety**

- pains

- feelings of being out of control, overwhelmed and incapable of coping

- a tendency to take risks

- use of alcohol or drugs instead of seeking the depression treatment

- loss of the libido

- changes in appetite

- lack of sleeping

- feelings of disconnection and isolation from partner, family or friends

Why fathers might feel stress in pregnancy

Money problems, relationships, and work pressures can all generate a lot of stress for men who are expecting a baby. Becoming a father entails a lot of transition - often all at once. You may be afraid about becoming the family's primary breadwinner, or you may believe you are unprepared to care for a newborn. You might also be concerned about 'losing' time with your partner or sharing your lover's attention and affection with a child.

The effect of father's stress on the partner and baby

You may believe you're managing your stress or that it's simply 'your issue.' However, too much stress can make you unhappy, and it might affect your relationships with others. You may be irritable and tense among others, as well as more prone to argue with your partner. If you use alcohol, cigarettes, or drugs to cope with stress, you may find that you are using them more frequently than usual. This can exacerbate tensions and arguments. If your stress levels become too high, your pregnant partner may become stressed as well. Unfortunately, this can also have an impact on your baby's health and development. Premature birth, low birth weight, and developmental delay are all connected to stress in pregnant women. Severe stress in pregnant women, which can be caused by things like divorce, family conflict, family violence, or poverty, can harm your baby's brain development and other areas of development. Stress can have a long-term impact on your child's emotions and behavior.

How to deal with stress in pregnancy

Ignoring your stress isn't going to make it go away. It can exacerbate the situation for you and those around you. It's good for you, your partner, and your kid to find strategies to cope with life's challenges. You could begin by gaining a better understanding of what to expect. When you're prepared and know what to expect in the first few months with your new kid, the impacts of stress aren't as terrible. You can learn by reading baby and parenting books, discussing your concerns with your partner, family, or friends who are new dads, and attending a birth class designed just for men, if one is available in your area. It's a good idea to talk to individuals you trust about the things that are causing you stress. This can be difficult because guys have few opportunities to interact with people. Many males find it difficult to express their concerns and emotions. Sharing what's going on can help you get clear on the genuine problems and solutions if you can get through the pain or awkwardness. If you're worried about financially supporting your family, for example, you may ask another father how he copes with being the breadwinner, if that's his experience. He might be able to offer some advice or insight. You might also get down to business and create a budget. This could be an excellent place to start with your partner when it comes to addressing your spending habits as well as work arrangements.

Things a woman can do

Preparing for a new born is a thrilling experience. However, making preparations for such a significant change in one's life, and dealing with the symptoms of physical pregnancy, could be daunting. Throughout pregnancy or the very first year following childbirth, up to one in every five women experiences mental health issues. Anxiety, depression, and low mood are all frequent. It's critical to look after your emotional as well as your own physical wellness. Here are methods to relax during your pregnancy.

Mindfulness

Do you always become engrossed in your own worries and concerns? Or maybe you're just undergoing the process of the day and have completely forgotten to appreciate the small pleasures in life? Take a moment to notice your moods, physical sensations, & the surroundings all around you. Mindfulness is all about being aware of what is happening outside and inside of oneself at any given time. It can assist you in staying in the current moment and minimizing anxieties. It can also assist you to connect with your own unborn baby while you're pregnant.

Pregnancy yoga

Yoga is a form of exercise that promotes both physical and mental well-being. Yoga is a terrific method to stay all active when pregnant, bolster your physique, and get rid of pains and aches. It can also be utilized to help you handle pain and bring your baby into ideal position during an active birth by using breathing positions and techniques. If you're new to the yoga, start with a class designed for pregnant females and wait till you're 14 weeks pregnant to begin. Yoga courses frequently conclude with a session of meditation, which can be really beneficial if you're stressed. Yoga classes once a week can help with depression and anxiety during pregnancy.

Complementary therapies

There are numerous complementary therapies which are safe to use during pregnancy, but check with your midwife first. A massage tailored to the needs of pregnant women may help to relieve stress. However, you should not have one during the first three pregnancy months because your stomach must not be massaged. Many individuals find out reflexology to be extremely calming. This massage is based upon the premise that reflex spots on the hands, feet, and head correspond to other body areas. We don't know if herbal medicines are risk-free to consume during pregnancy, so avoid them.

Exercise

Exercising is safe during pregnancy. It is, in fact, incredibly beneficial and strongly recommended. It may also not sound appealing, particularly if you're sick, exhausted, or overweight. But believe us, taking relaxing swims or regular mild walks can help your baby, your body, and your labor.

Chapter 5: Ensure Smooth Transition into Fatherhood

Whether you're still reeling from the news or have been anticipating it for years, learning you're going to be a parent is a life-changing experience. Even if this is something you've always desired, it's natural to feel a range of emotions, from sheer excitement to outright horror. It's difficult to ever feel totally prepared to become a father.

5.1 Steps to take at work to ensure a smooth transition into fatherhood

We've got some suggestions for you as you prepare for the arrival of your child, as well as for the exciting-yet-tiresome, exhilarating-yet-exhausting months ahead.

Start your research

You may not be carrying the baby physically, but that doesn't mean you aren't a part of the pregnancy and birth process. The same may be said for individuals who are utilizing a surrogate or adopting a child – there are many ways to participate. There are plenty of books produced specifically for expectant fathers, but you don't have to stick to them. Join an online support group or subscribe to a pregnancy newsletter. If your spouse is having pregnancy symptoms such as morning sickness or heartburn, you'll need to conduct some research to figure out what's causing it. Knowing what they're going through can help you better assist them while they're carrying your child. Knowing what to expect when it comes to labor, birth, and caring for a newborn can make the entire process a lot easier. You'll need to learn about vaginal and cesarean births, breastfeeding, diaper changes, and other topics.

Get healthy

It's a great time to focus on your personal health before your kid arrives. If you smoke, make an effort to stop. Smoking during pregnancy has been linked to an increased risk of congenital cardiac abnormalities in babies. What kind of eating habits do you have? Now is the time to start eating wisely to fuel your long days (and nights) as a new parent. Consider making these healthy replacements if your diet could benefit from a few tweaks. Alternatively, include some fiber-rich, immune-boosting foods in your diet.

Talk about parenting with your co-parent

Now is an excellent time to begin talking about the type of parents you want to be. Are you both interested in breastfeeding? Breastfeeding success requires the father's support. Do you want your child to sleep in their own room in a crib as soon as you come home? Will you both be working? What are your daycare plans? Keep in mind that these are still hypothetical situations for both of you. Your feelings may alter once the baby arrives. Breastfeeding may be more difficult than you anticipated, and you may want to reconsider your emotions toward cloth diapering. There will be certain discussions that aren't immediately relevant, but are nonetheless significant. Discipline, including spanking, should be discussed before your child becomes a rowdy toddler. Starting the conversation now allows you to open those channels of communication and get on the same parenting page.

Start playing as a team

When we talk about being on the exact page, we're referring to the fact that now is the time to start thinking of selves as a team. Even if your romantic connection with your co-parent ends, you, your co-parent, and your child are forever intertwined. Starting to see things through that lens and letting go of keeping score as if you were in a competition is a wonderful approach. If the person carrying your child is weary and experiencing morning sickness, assisting them will benefit both you and your baby. You can support your common goal – caring for your family — by feeding them what they can eat, picking up the slack on housekeeping, or ensuring to check in on them every day.

Decide on the father you want to be

Some people have strained relations with their own father. If you're fortunate enough to have a good father, you may aspire to be just like him — and that's fantastic. If your own father left a lot to be desired, you might be concerned about taking on the role of a father. The good news is that you have complete control over how you approach parenthood. Look for fathers who can serve as role models for you. You're creating this role from the scratch, and it's up to you to decide how it should look.

Find fellow dads

On that subject, finding some other fathers for your friend group is fantastic. Having someone who understands the difficulties of parenthood gives you an opportunity and a place to ask questions, vent, or empathize about your new role as a father. There are internet groups, church groups, and organizations that your doctor or hospital can refer you to.

Go to the appointments whenever you can

Prenatal appointments are a fantastic opportunity to get excited about the upcoming pregnancy. Of course, seeing the baby-to-be on ultrasound is an unforgettable event, but even routine checks may help you connect with the pregnancy as well as learn more about what to expect. You'll be able to ask your own questions, discover more about your baby's development, and find out what your partner is going through. While work schedules and other obstacles may prohibit you from attending every visit, speak with your co-

parent about developing a schedule that permits you to attend as many as possible. When the baby is the one who is booked for newborn checkups, this can continue.

Acknowledge your sex life may change

Being a parent can have a significant impact on your sexual life. You can feel passionately attached to your partner and crave the intimacy of sex from the moment you find they're expecting, anxious about doing anything that could harm the pregnancy, or simply... puzzled. This is another situation in which open communication is essential. Many jokes will be made about how your sex life is over, or about the physical changes that occur during pregnancy. These remarks are unhelpful because they neglect the emotional complexities of sex and parenthood. The truth is that sex after pregnancy takes time — and we're not just talking about the recommended 6-week recovery period for physical healing following labor and delivery. It's critical to be aware of all the changes you're going through as a couple - lack of sleep, breastfeeding, the emotional toll of having a newborn — and to talk with your partner about their and your own intimacy and sexual requirements. Sex after a baby, on the other hand, can be much better. You're connected in ways you've never been before, and many couples find that being parents brings them even closer together.

Celebrate the milestones

The focus of pregnancy development and celebrations such as baby showers is often on the pregnant person, but you are also a part of this. Consider throwing a co-ed shower so you may participate in

the fun. Choose items for your baby with your partner while shopping. Keep a journal of your thoughts and feelings. Take a lot of pictures of yourself throughout the pregnancy. It's just as crucial for you to keep track of these life changes.

Embrace your place in the preparations

There's a lot to accomplish in order to get ready for a new baby. Carrying the baby isn't the only consideration. To prepare for your newborn, you will need to create a registry, prepare a room, save money, study child care, and many other tasks. You might discover that you enjoy participating in all of the tasks or that you're better suited to handle only a few of them. Look for a variety of methods to get involved in the preparations for your new arrival. You must learn how to install and use the car seat (and volunteer to teach others), make phone calls about childcare or insurance, assemble furniture or paint the room, research the best baby carriers or formula, attend a birth or breastfeeding class with your partner, discuss your leave options with your employer, and learn to prepare and pack the hospital bag.

Act as the communicator when needed

A new baby may bring out the best in people – as well as the worst. Do you recall the conversation concerning your team? You, your co-parent, and your new baby are the only ones in the room. It's up to your team to select who will attend the birth, how soon you'll welcome guests, and a million other details. It's critical that you speak up if relatives or friends dispute your decisions. It's important to remember that setting boundaries is healthy and acceptable. It's fine if you want to celebrate your baby's birth by inviting everyone you know to your home in the days after his or her arrival. However, if you want to minimize visitors and spend some quality time with your family alone, it is also a terrific option. You can be the one to inform others about what you and your family will and will not be doing.

Advocate for your co-parent

This may entail speaking up during appointments or during childbirth. This could entail doing everything you can to assist them in their decision to return to work — or to remain at home. This could also entail seeing indicators of postpartum depression and assisting them in seeking professional help. You're a great force in their health's support. Having two healthy parents is also beneficial to your child.

Share responsibilities

We discussed this throughout pregnancy, but make sure you continue to be involved once the kid is born. In the early days, it's easy for fathers to feel left out, especially if the other parent is breastfeeding. You could think your position isn't as significant as others', but it is. You may take care of your infant by changing diapers not only during the day but also at night. You must learn how to bathe your newborn. To assist in building a safe relationship, you must spend time skin-to-skin. Reading to your child is a good idea. You should sing a beautiful song before going to bed. You must be prepared to bottle feed, or if your baby is solely breastfed, you must show concern for them before and after meals. You should provide drinks and food for your co-parent. You should be prepared to undertake household duties such as dishes and laundry, and you can baby wear while doing so.

Keep your sense of humor

Parenting is a messy business. It's difficult, confusing, and draining. It is, however, enjoyable, exciting, and fulfilling. Being able to laugh through both happy and bad times is crucial to getting through them. When you haven't had enough sleep and every diaper seems to be a blowout, and you spill breast milk in your coffee, your ability to laugh will get you through the difficulties.

Sleep

Your companion is in desperate need of sleep. You require rest. Your child requires rest. There are different techniques for sleeping, and finding the ideal one for your family may take some trial and error. What matters is that everyone gets some rest. You may have to work tomorrow, but your co-parent does as well. Sleep in shifts, nap whenever you can, and divide and conquer jobs and responsibilities that need to be completed so the other person can relax. Ensure that everyone in the house has a chance to sleep, no matter what you do.

Know you're important to your baby

There will be several stages in the life of your child. You could feel unconnected or unimportant at times. Returning to work or feeling like a secondary caregiver can be challenging. Working outside the home for a living, on the other hand, does not make you a bad parent; you are providing for your family. Trust us when we say that you'll have plenty of opportunities to shine, such as when your child says "dada" or grips your finger for the first time. When you're the only one around, they might want you to tuck them in or sing them a song. It's all about being in it for the long run when it comes to fatherhood. Every day, you give them — and yourself — a gift by being there in their lives.

Chapter 6: Learn to Manage the First Six Months of Your Baby

The development of an infant starts at birth. Your infant will grow quickly and understand a lot at first. The following are some suggestions for managing the first six months of your baby's life.

6.1 Tips for managing the one-month old baby

At one month, all your baby cares about is sleeping, cuddling, and eating. As they begin to encounter the world, the time you put in with them will aid in the growth & development of their brain. Your infant will most likely be crying so much right now. Often, it's because they have a dirty nappy or hungry, but babies scream for no visible reason as well. To console them, give lots of cuddles and reassure them that the crying period will pass. At one month, they should be able to focus both eyes and from side to side, accompany a moving object. They will most likely prefer staring at a human being's face over seeing at an item, and if you have them in your hands around 45 centimeters away, they will look intently into your eyes. By this age, most newborns can recognize their parents. Babies who are one month old enjoy hearing your words, but if they notice a loud kind of noise, they will be startled. They may recoil and stretch their legs and arms, blink their eyes, & exhale more quickly. Some newborns will learn to comfort themselves with the dummy or by sucking their thumbs or fingers at the age of one month. It's a good idea to help your baby suck to make them feel better. Spend more time with your baby as possible. Looking them in the eyes and grinning will aid them attach and feel protected and comfortable. Read to your child & sing to him or her. Even if they don't comprehend what you're saying, they'll like listening to your voice. Music stimulates their sensations and keeps them engaged. Playing games along with them can also assist to strengthen your bond. Put your baby on their stomach for one to five minutes at the time to help them develop neck strength. This is referred to as tummy time. During tummy time, keep your eye on your baby & always place them on their backs to sleep.

6.2 Tips for managing the two months old baby

You'll notice that your baby is awake more during the day as they create a rhythm. This allows you to spend more time with them and assist them in their development. Spend a lot of time reading to them, singing to them, and talking with them. They will become accustomed to sounds and words and will begin to build language and communication abilities in this manner. You can engage them in play by allowing them to examine and feel a range of objects of various designs, colors, and shapes. Soft balls and plastic toys work well. They will like staring at you, so make an effort to smile at them frequently. It makes your infant feel safe and comfortable by releasing 'feel-good' hormones in their bodies. You could also massage your infant to help them calm. It's a good time after a bath. To strengthen their neck and upper body, continue with 1 to 5 minutes of tummy time. It will aid in the development of the muscles they will need to sit and crawl later. However, always place your infant to sleep on his or her back.

6.3 Tips for managing the three months old baby

The foundations of language are being laid at this time. As much as possible, talk and read to your baby. It will assist them in understanding how language works and how conversations flow. Encourage your baby to express by responding to him or her with words or varied noises. Choose baby books with large, colorful illustrations. It doesn't really matter what you say; what matters is the tone of your voice. Tell your baby the names of items around them by pointing to them. It's fine to use both languages to describe the world to your kid if you live in a multilingual household. When your baby is on their tummy, dangle a toy in front of them to help them build the muscles in their neck and back. Alternatively, give them a toy to assist them in learning to hold it. Stroke them with various materials such as fur, felt, and tissue to stimulate their sense of touch. Cuddles, massages, and moving them around in the air can all help them relax.

6.4 Tips for managing the four months old baby

Continue to speak and read to your child to assist them learn language and communication. To emphasize the story, use varied tones and intonations in your voice, as well as distinct facial expressions. Singing songs, reading books, playing with toys, and listening to you make funny noises are all things your baby will enjoy. Developing a routine will benefit your baby. Do things in a similar way every day if it works for both of you. This will give them a sense of safety and security. It's also a good idea to start thinking about how you'll prepare your home once they start moving around. It might happen at any time.

6.5 Tips for managing the five months old baby

Talk to your baby and pay attention to him or her. Respond to the sounds they create with varying tones and facial emotions. This enables them to gain a better understanding of how conversations work and how to convey their emotions. Read books to your baby, sing to them, give them tummy time, make funny noises, and give them toys as much as possible. They may be too tired or hungry to play at times, but you should be able to pick up on your baby's cues by now, so make sure you give them what they require.

6.6 Tips for managing the six months old baby

Your child will enjoy discovering the world. Surround them with safe items that they can handle and put in their mouth, such as a soft ball, various fabrics, teething rings, or bells. Look your infant in the eyes, make facial expressions, and respond to their sounds while you talk and listen to them. They will like being read to, especially books with colorful pictures. Enjoy this unique moment with them by cuddling while you read to them. When they're around people they don't know, reassure them to make them feel protected and secure. Now is the moment to baby proof your home, if you haven't already. Your kid will be on the move shortly, so make sure their surroundings are secure.

Chapter 7: Learn to Manage the Relationship with Father and Mother

Children who have a positive relationship with their parents are more likely to form positive relationships with others. They can form strong relationships and friendships with their peers. When presented with stress or a challenging scenario, they are better at controlling their emotions.

7.1 Importance of positive parent-child relationships

When children have strong, caring, good relationships with their parents & other caregivers, they learn and develop more effectively. This is because strong child-parent relationships help children gain knowledge about the world — if it is secure and safe, whether they are loved and by whom, what occurs when they laugh, cry, or pull a face, and etc. Being present with your child, choosing to spend time with the children, and creating a trusting, kind, and respectful environment are all methods to foster a positive relation with your child.

7.2 How to manage connection with your father and mother

A careful balance is required in the relationship between children and parents. Roles can shift considerably throughout the span of a lifetime. For everyone concerned, this can be a cause of stress at times. Adult children frequently lose touch with parents as they getting older and are no more reliant on them for almost all of their needs. However, every attempt should be taken to maintain this positive relationship. Here are few pointers to help you improve your relations with your parents.

Look towards your parents as the adults

As children grow into adults and parents age, it is hard to shift the dynamic of the child/ parent relation. Preventing the connection from evolving, on the other hand, might strangle it. You must behave like the adult while you are with your parents if you want them to see you as an adult. Ask yourself whether you would treat your friend or colleague differently in the exact situation to ensure you are treating your parents like adults. You're on the correct track if you answered "yes." If the answer to that is "no," make the necessary adjustments to your behavior.

Maintain your sense of humor

When dealing with ageing parents as your parent adult child, it's natural to grow frustrated. Maintaining your humor can help you and your parents relax. Look for humor in the everyday events and also more unusual challenges that arise. Have a stock of jokes on hand so you could crack a joke whenever the scenario calls for it.

Talk to your parents about your concerns

Even if your parents' activities drive you insane, be honest with them. If you bottle up your bad emotions, they can rapidly turn into resentment, that can be detrimental to your relationship. Connect your feelings in a respectful and gentle manner.

Don't forget to thank your parents for everything they do for you

Despite the fact that you are an adult and live by yourself, you still require the assistance of your parents. Mother may no longer prepare your food or do your laundry, and father may no more be the mechanic for your vehicle. However, your parents can still assist you in a variety of ways. For instance, your mother may become your go-to nanny (at no cost), or your father could provide you a lift to & from the work while your car is inside the shop. Even though you don't count on your parents for so much, when you come home to visit, your mother will make your preferred cookies. It's crucial to express your gratitude for their assistance, whether it's significant or simply an unrequested-for gesture of compassion.

Share similar interests

You & your parents are likely to share identical hobbies. They are the individuals who taught you everything you know regarding your favorite hobbies and sports. Spend time with your parents talking about instances when you & your parents had similar interests. Make time to create new memories by rekindling your interest in these pastimes. Also, talk with your parents to observe if you have any new common interests that you did not have when you were a youngster.

Allow them to have some independence

The child/parent relationship takes a long time to change. We require less caring from our parents as we mature and become the adults. Breaking those ties, on the other hand, can be tough. Keep an eye on your own actions and don't rely onto your parents to fix all of your issues. Your parents will forever be there for you, but there are occasions when their own requirements must take precedence in their lives. Even when our parents become older and require more assistance, we must avoid behaving with them like children and give them the freedom to do everyday duties on their own.

Recognize your differences from your parents.

Regardless of the reality that you were raised by your parents, you are likely to be dissimilar from them in some significant ways. You must understand that parting ways with your parents and having your own beliefs and ideas is an important aspect of growing up. When it comes to areas where you disagree with your parents, they can be touchy matters that generate problems once they are brought up. However, acknowledging these all differences and accepting that the both your and your parents' perspectives are acceptable and okay is an important aspect of becoming an adult and having a successful relation with your parents. Maintain a good and healthy relationship with your parents. Among the most important relationships in your life is your mature relationship with your parents. Take the time to look after it and treat it with the love and respect it deserves.

Manage relationships with your father and mother's parents

You need to give them equal respect and show your love and affection for them. You must not neglect any one of them and invite them to all your family functions lest they feel neglected. You also need to ensure that your father and mother manifest respect, love and affection for each other parents. You should consult each one of them during any challenging situation or seek their advice on a particular subject. This will go a long way in establishing healthy family relationships and staving off any disputes.

Conclusion

Few things have almost the same impact on a man's life as becoming a dad. Being charged with another person's care and responsibility is a huge responsibility, but nothing compares to becoming a father and witnessing your child develop into an adult, with your affection reciprocated and your child's self-worth reaffirmed. The craft of fatherhood evolves in tandem with society and the traditional family. While learning how to be a more supportive, involved, and loving father, fathers may help their children build self-esteem and confidence. In today's society, single-parent families, blended families, unmarried parents, parents of the same gender, & multi-generational families are becoming more prevalent. Cultural changes such as the spike in the amount of women working outside their home, remarriages, increased rates of divorce, and mixed families have resulted in shifts in mother and paternal obligations over the previous three decades. Ask any modern father about his father-son or father-daughter relationships, and he'll tell you that they're nothing like the ones he had to his own father.

As a consequence of changes in parenting techniques, men today have more alternatives for responding to their obligations as fathers, wives, or partners. Today's father is much less likely to attract fatherhood guidance from his own upbringing. Because dads' roles evolve over time, what functioned well for his father thirty years ago might no longer work with today's complicated and varied difficulties. According to a new analysis, fathers who are polite &

tolerant are more likely to have self-esteem in their children. A loving and caring father-child relationship aids in the development of peer popularity, children's success, and personal adjustment. Children benefit from fathers who provide suitable, consistent guidance without pushing their will on them. You need to actually spend time with your child. How a father spends his own time shows what matters to him to his child. Children are swiftly growing up, and now is the greatest time to spend time with them. All kids require proper discipline and supervision, not as a punishment form but as a way of setting realistic limits. Dads must remind their children of the results of their actions & reward good behavior. Fathers who actually discipline their kids in a peaceful and equitable manner show that they care about them. As a parent, you must set an example for your child. For their children, fathers serve as role models. A girl that spends more time with caring father understands what to search for in a partner and that she is deserving of respect from boys. By demonstrating humility, honesty, and accountability, fathers model what is vital in life for girls and boys. Fathers should begin talking to the children about important issues while they are younger so that difficult issues can be dealt with more easily as they get older. Take a moment to hear your child's concerns and views. Teach your children the difference between wrong and right, and encourage them to strive to be the good parents. Ascertain that your children make sound decisions. Actively involved fathers teach their kids life skills through everyday examples. Dinners with the family are an important section of maintaining a good family life. It enables kids to talk regarding what they're doing and also what they like to do. It's also an excellent opportunity for the fathers to participate and pay attention. It provides a plan for the families to follow so that they can spend quality time together often. Fathers must make efforts to read out to their own children in a culture dominated by the internet and television in order to raise lifelong readers. Begin reading to them when actually they are small, and as they get older, push them to read independently.

Instilling a passion for reading in kids is one of the most successful ways for ensuring their literacy and professional and personal growth for a lifetime. You must respect the other parent of your child. Respectful parents that exhibit mutual appreciation for their children provide a safe environment for their children. When children see their parents respecting one other, they are more likely to feel welcomed and respected in the father-child relationship. A good parent instils in his child a sense of safety and security. He has the ability to protect his children from any harm. A good father is also aware of how to hold the bad guys at bay.

Most importantly, a good father is always concerned about his mother. For good fathers, early engagement is critical. Learn about a father's responsibility throughout adoption, pregnancy, or surrogacy, and gently touch, play, hold, and talk to your infant kid to demonstrate early engagement. It sends a strong and unambiguous message when fathers are involved: "I'd like to adopt you as a child. I'm intrigued by you, and our friendship is quite important to me."

Finally, if you found this book useful in any way, a review on Amazon is always appreciated!

Thank you.

John Riley

Printed in Great Britain
by Amazon

13983346R00059